SIMPLE, GREEN PEST AND DISEASE CONTROL

SIMPLE, GREEN PEST AND DISEASE CONTROL

·Bob Flowerdew·

Kyle Cathie Limited

First published in Great Britain in 2010 by
Kyle Cathie Limited
23 Howland Street
London, W1T 4AY
www.kylecathie.com

Text 2010 © Bob Flowerdew
Design 2010 © Kyle Cathie Limited
Photography 2010 © Peter Cassidy
Illustration 2010 © Alison Clements

ISBN 978-1-85626-928-5

10 9 8 7 6 5 4 3 2 1

A Cataloguing in Publication record for this title
is available from the British Library.

Photography: Peter Cassidy
Illustrations: Alison Clements
Design: Louise Leffler
Project Editor: Sophie Allen
Copy Editor: Helena Caldon

Photographic Acknowledgements:
All photography by Peter Cassidy except
pp. 38, 95, 96, 104, 109 by Fran Yorke and
p. 52 by Bob Flowerdew

Printed in China by 1010 Printing International Ltd

Contents

Introduction

Some see gardening as a war against pests and diseases, however, there is another way: to harness nature using the natural checks and balances for our purposes – that is, to control the pests and diseases. And it is only control we are after, not eradication. Even if it were possible to eliminate any single one of them, it would only be temporary as they would soon be back. A pest outbreak in your garden will probably be repeated in every other one up and down the land. There are bad years with aphids everywhere, then other, good years with ladybirds everywhere and few aphids evident. We cannot escape from the vast majority of common woes, but we can minimise their damage and annoyance. And rather than throw poisons about ineffectually, we can use our wit and cunning to outmanoeuvre problems using simple greener methods.

Gardeners have always been good at observing, working out what is happening; then finding ingenious ways of altering it. Most of the cunning ideas in this book were conceived by countless gardeners before now, but as so few rely on some 'product', many have not been widely publicised. Each is not an 'immediate solution', with a pile of corpses proving its efficacy. Here we are merely shifting the balance, not eradicating the enemy. There is not just one answer but a range of controls we can employ. We create multiple layers of defence to win the battle for our flowers, fruits and vegetables despite the pests and diseases, by thwarting rather than eliminating them.

And we have a huge advantage; we can be ready forewarned so that each year we can take actions before known problems arise. For example: by covering your carrots with fine-mesh netting after sowing, you prevent carrot root flies reaching them to lay their eggs, so they are forced to go elsewhere and will lay them fruitlessly on the compost heap where you have lain some carefully bruised carrot leaves to lure them.

There is a huge range of acceptable and efficient controls for most pests and diseases and it is up to us to employ those most suitable to our particular circumstances. And we should choose not just one but a selection of those that have already proved most effective. Then we can rest content that our hard work will come to fruition.

Why exercise pest and disease control?

The classic responses are that, without control, we experience unacceptable loss of yields or damage that spoils the pristine appearance of our plants. This is indeed true; not only do pests rob us of crops or flowers directly, or indirectly by weakening the plant, but others spread diseases, causing further damage. The big bud mite of blackcurrants does not just destroy the fruit buds it infests, but carries a reversion virus which cripples them so the yields drop irreversibly. Some pests and diseases are devastating, such as gooseberry sawfly which, when left unchecked, may totally defoliate a bush, or potato blight which wipes out whole crops overnight, countywide.

Right: Without prompt control, sawfly caterpillars could strip off every leaf

Sometimes you have no choice but to tackle the pests. In some countries, there are laws demanding you report or treat certain pests or diseases, that you must control others and you are forbidden to import or grow some plants because these may encourage problems. For example, in the UK you must report Colorado beetles (yellow 'ladybirds' scoffing your potatoes), prune out and burn plum branches with Silver leaf disease, and you may not plant Laxton's Superb pear, as it is prone to fireblight – a widespread fungal disease. In some US states, berberis was banned as it was thought to carry wheat rust, and blackcurrants are banned in others.

One reason why so much spraying was done in the past was because of a fear that problems would get worse and would spread to everything else. Although a very few pests, such as slugs or rabbits, may attack almost anything, most are very specific about their diet and seldom move to unrelated plants. Even fewer diseases spread widely as they are often specific to certain plants. However, you can understand the fear; some years everything starts to get mildew or rust, but that's because the season favours them – hollyhock rust does not move to leeks, it's just that both suffer their own version at the same time. Better prediction of when diseases such as potato blight are probable, for example in warm moist weather, at least allows a reduction of controls at less risky times.

Because common pests and diseases often attack popular plants, one way to avoid many of them is to grow the rare and unusual rather than the commonplace. There are far more pests and diseases for radishes, roses and rhododendrons than for aronia, arbutus and artichokes.

Left: A fruit cage makes more difference than all other pest and disease controls put together

Why not to control at all

If you cast your eyes around almost any flower garden, at first glance all usually appears well. Look closer, though, and you will find that almost every plant has some minor damage, but overall these minor defects do not seriously dent their appearance or yields. Although you're not deliberately exerting much control, inadvertently you have done so by creating a rich diversity of plants; far more variety of flowering plants than you'd find in the same area in untrammelled nature. With these plants supporting a diversity of life, you get much more passive control. Basically, although pests are there, there are also many things looking for lunch who control them for you.

So, simply because of the wide range of ornamentals we grow and the diversity of wildlife attracted to them, these are inherently easier to keep 'clean' than the vegetables and fruits. Likewise, few diseases infect them, usually affecting but one or two, whereas because so many vegetables and fruits are closely related they may suffer more as diseases and pests spread amongst them rather easily. However, even so, seldom does one reach epidemic proportions.

An important reason not to rush into excessive control is that, often, if we get anything at all we get a glut. Much of growing is in the teeth of the weather. There are good years and bad years; the pests make less difference than the season. Of course, in a bad year you do not want your few apples to be full of holes. However, most years most trees give a huge surplus of apples of which those with holes are only a small proportion of a surplus anyway. Likewise with runner beans, the problem is getting them to germinate in a cold year and to grow a foot or two out of the ground, so pests and diseases may be irrelevant by comparison. More attention to watering and warmth, and prompt picking, make much bigger differences to the total harvest. Indeed, by far the worst losses come from inclement weather, ill-advised choices and wrong methods, ineffectual picking and harvesting, and poor storage.

Right: Apples can crop so heavily, even a happy goose can't make a dent in them

Seasons are good and bad. In some years, everybody has ripe tomatoes and we all suffer bird damage, in others everyone has blight and we all have rotten tomatoes. The pests and diseases are as much controlled by good and bad seasons as the plants. There are dry years and slug and snail years. We can even predict some problems even before they appear – any summer period of warm and wet will have slug and snail and blight problems. Conversely, when the weather is dry and hot, then soon there are aphids, rusts and mildews everywhere.

Then there are the natural cycles of control. When there are many aphids, so their controls, such as ladybirds and lacewings, multiply. Eventually there are not enough aphids to go round, the controls die, and the surviving aphids multiply again. There are, thus, natural cycles of aphid years then ladybird years, and both interact with the weather. If we intervene, we disrupt the process locally, but probably in favour of the pests. This is simply because pests are in bigger numbers and breed much faster than predators or parasites. If we spray wide-scale poisons about and kill, say, 99.9 per cent of everything, still an aphid or two in nooks somewhere will doubtless escape, but likely no ladybirds.

Why not let nature take its course? Because nature will reach a balance but probably too late to save this year's crops or flowers. So we need to intervene, but cautiously, with the least damage to these natural checks and balances. Ideally, this should be done with passive defences such as nets, fleeces and cloches, which serve our needs without risking the ecosystem. (Except, of course, in their manufacture, transport, etc., etc.)

In some cases, a pest even does us a favour. Leaf-blistering aphid damage rarely affects yield in redcurrants though it looks disastrous, so it can be ignored and the insects will convert into ladybirds to control aphids elsewhere. Likewise, the cherry aphis effectively summer prunes for us by withering back the ends of shoots and leaves.

A reasonable level of damage can be acceptable. Perfection is needed commercially and 'for show', but most gardeners accept some damage if the bulk of the crop escapes. Likewise, if you want roses to cut for the table, it matters not a jot that half their leaves have been sculpted by leaf cutter bees.

Left: Warm wet nights and you can catch these by torchlight

And most established plants can sustain an awful lot of apparent damage to little real detriment. If, say, a quarter of all leaves are nibbled away, the light falls more intensely on those left that were previously in the shade of others. It is small and young plants that need most care and protection; once they are larger and established, most plants will go on to give flowers or crops despite attacks, albeit possibly in slightly diminished quantity. But if you have a surplus anyway, what's it matter?

Plant hypochondria. As with human health, there is a difference between sensible concern and frequent panic. It is better to err on the side of caution, not interfering, than to rush to actions for which there is little or no need. Likewise, it helps to know a plant's normal appearance and their seasonal changes. Quite often, novice gardeners believe they have potato blight when it's just the normal dying back of early varieties – it's what they do. It's also possible to confuse deficiency and disease; the rightly feared raspberry mosaic virus with mottling of the leaves can be misdiagnosed from inter-veinal yellowing caused by dry alkaline soils (which would be easily rectified with mulches of leaf-mould).

Plant vitality, age and damage. The basic rule is that the smaller and younger the plant, the more it must be cosseted. It is the seedlings and newer leaves that slugs and most pests go for; aphids likewise generally infest the younger shoots. Once leaves and shoots are older they become tougher and less palatable, thus the vegetable bed with its annual crops is again much more prey to pests than, say, the shrub border where we seldom need to practise much control. Diseases strike plants that are least able to resist so, once more, the vegetables, which are highly developed and under strain, suffer more than the majority of ornamentals which are frequently tougher wild forms.

At some point, although you may be able to deal with a pest or disease problem, you have to ask is it worth the effort? Why expend a lot of

Above: For clean roses for cutting, squirt
aphids off the fattening buds with a jet of water

work to stop blight on outdoor tomatoes in September when frost is going to have them soon anyway? Or is it just too late? Many of the less commonly occurring problems are only ever spotted when it is too late to make much effective difference. There's no point saving a badly nibbled crop of rocket or radish when it's simpler, and the results better, to sow another batch elsewhere.

Recognise the incurable. Most problems with a chemical solution have a green alternative but some are insoluble either way. There are no cures for virus diseases that plague strawberry, raspberry and blackcurrant plants; if they contract these they can only be eradicated. Likewise, few measures will discourage two-legged rats, birds and badgers from robbing us, and worse there are laws preventing the few effective old-fashioned ways of dealing with them.

Timing is everything, so for a control to work it needs to be in place before the problem occurs. Net your crops before birds start on them or they'll persist in trying. Wasp traps need to catch the first scouts, then if these don't return, the armies will not arrive until much later. You see your new transplants developing holes, do nothing and they are going to become more damaged as the slugs return each evening. So go out the first nights with a torch and there they are waiting to be picked off! Every gardener should make night-time patrols at least fortnightly during the growing season.

Our great advantage over pests and diseases, as I drew to your attention earlier, is our ability to be forewarned and so take pre-emptive action. Keep a diary – note when you first spotted a problem and on what. For sure, over the next years it may recur, and within a week or two of the same date, so on perusing the months ahead you can plan to take whatever actions are necessary to thwart them. For example, if mildew appears on your gooseberries most Junes, make a note to prune hard and open up the plant in winter, to give them wood ash and to mulch in spring, and to water heavily during May; then the mildew will probably never happen.

Left: Panic not: with normal seasonal decay, the plant may be suffering, but cold will finish it off in another week or two anyway

Know your

There are doubtless hundreds of potential pests and diseases for any garden, but only a few commonly plague us. It is against these few that we must make most effort, as their appearance is almost guaranteed. Only a fool would not expect birds to eat their strawberries or their beetroot and spinach seedlings. In these cases, no control can equal almost no crop. Each garden suffers more or less from common problems, though you may escape rabbits but have badgers, or have few slugs but many caterpillars. It helps to refine your controls if you know who your worst enemies are so, when you spot their depredations, you know what you can best do about them. After the commonest offenders listed overleaf – in my grievance order – are the ten lines of defence from page 33. Each one has methods that work far better for one challenge than another. Ideally, employ as many layers of defence as possible.

Right: It's the early bird gets the worm, and your raspberries, and your beetroot seedlings...

enemy

Pests

Wood pigeons – they trample everything and especially devour brassicas, salads and peas. See Fourth: Barriers (page 48), Tenth: Direct action (page 102).

Blackbirds and others – If seed, seedlings and fruit are gone, note triangular holes. See Fourth: Barriers, Tenth: Direct action.

Deer – Graze from knee high to above their heads, eating bark and foliage. See Fourth: Barriers, Tenth: Direct action.

Badgers – Cause vandalism and chaos on a grand scale. See Fourth: Barriers.

Foxes – Buried things will appear, pets and poultry will be missing and there will be holes in the lawn. See Fourth: Barriers, Sixth: Traps (page 66), Tenth: Direct action.

Rabbits – Look for vegetables and bedding neatly gone and bark damage. See Fourth: Barriers, Sixth: Traps, Tenth: Direct action.

Moles – These need no description. See Fourth: Barriers, Sixth: Traps, Tenth: Direct action. Hire a professional!

Cats – Cause odd nibble marks, flattened seedbeds, nasty flesh or foul presents. See Fourth: Barriers.

Dogs – Will make burn marks on the lawn, scratch up areas, and leave dead trees with a strange smell. See Fourth: Barriers, and give bitches tomato purée with their food as this reduces lawn burn – honest!

Rats and mice – Cause damage and loss to seeds, seedlings, stores, and make holes in the ground, in and under buildings with gnaw marks. The size of the droppings indicate which pest: raisins is rats, rice is mice. See Fourth: Barriers, Sixth: Traps, Tenth: Direct action.

(Special Note: rats and mice are such vermin, damaging and carrying disease that, as well

'You should not tolerate rats or mice, as they also spread disease, but you can turn a blind eye to moles and their annoying habits, as they carry no other problem.'

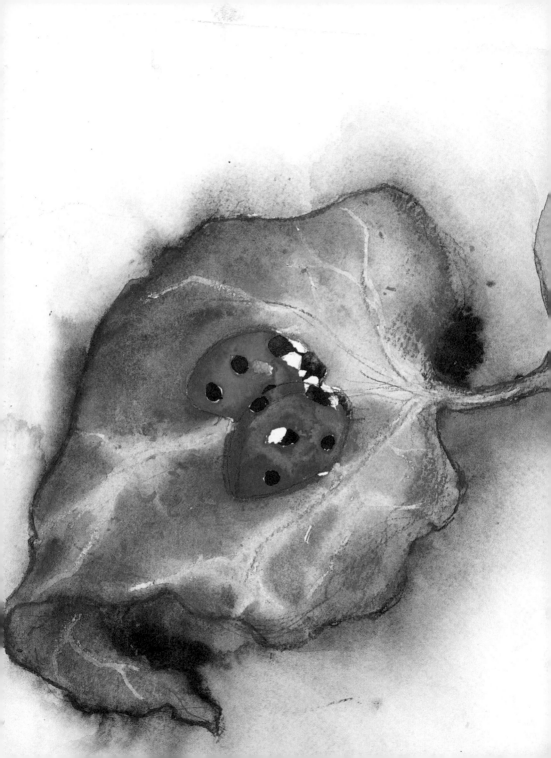

as traps, poisoning may be necessary. We have a duty to keep these under control and hire professionals or use commercial baits, exactly as stipulated, with all due precautions.)

Slugs and snails – Holes rasped into and onto leaves, tubers and fruits, missing seedlings and slime trails are evident. See Fourth: Barriers, Sixth: Traps, Seventh: Encourage natural predators (page 76), Ninth: Buying in biological controls (page 94), Tenth: Direct action.

Flatworms – When worms disappear, then drainage worsens, you may find these flattened slimey 'worms' hiding under stones and slabs. See Sixth: Traps, Seventh: Encourage natural predators, Tenth: Direct action.

Vine weevil – Noticed by notched holes in the edges of leaves and plants that are failing with their roots missing, grubs found in soil or compost nearby. See Fourth: Barriers, Sixth: Traps, Seventh: Encourage natural predators, Ninth: Buying in biological controls, Tenth: Direct action.

Wood lice, earwigs, millipedes – Shoots, seedlings, tubers and fruits will be damaged, and these pests in evidence. See Third: Cunning cultural methods (page 44), Fourth: Barriers, Sixth: Traps, Seventh: Encourage natural predators, Tenth: Direct action.

'There are so many cunning ways to neutralise pests that few should long trouble us.'

Left: Two ladybirds - soon there'll be many more - can't do that with bottles of spray

Caterpillars – These are most often evident, though leaves damaged or missing may indicate they're hiding or have dropped off. See Fourth: Barriers, Fifth: Hide and seek (page 62), Sixth: Traps, Seventh: Encourage natural predators, Eighth: Companion plants (page 86), Ninth: Buying in biological controls, Tenth: Direct action.

Grubs in fruits – The culprits are easily evident as small grubs, though often just the tunnels and exit holes remain. See Fourth: Barriers, Sixth: Traps, Seventh: Encourage natural predators, Ninth: Buying in biological controls, Tenth: Direct action.

Grubs in roots and tubers – These are evident from their holes and tunnels. See Second: Resistant varieties (page 41), Third: Cunning cultural methods, Fourth: Barriers, Fifth: Hide and seek, Sixth: Traps, Seventh: Encourage natural predators, Eighth: Companion plants, Ninth: Buying in biological controls, Tenth: Direct action.

Aphids (and the very similar Psyllids) – Little green, black or other coloured bugs can be seen, usually on shoot tips or leaf undersides, often with leaf curling. See First: Healthy plants (page 34), Second: Resistant varieties, Third: Cunning cultural methods, Fourth: Barriers, Fifth: Hide and seek, Sixth: Traps, Seventh: Encourage natural predators, Eighth: Companion plants, Ninth: Buying in biological controls, Tenth: Direct action.

Scale insects – Shrubs and trees indoors and out will get small helmet- or bud-like bumps on stems, often with powdery insides (eggs). See Ninth: Buying in biological controls, Tenth: Direct action (rub them off or cover with soft soap foam).

Vine weevils can only walk, not fly

Mealy bugs – An indoor problem of minute waxy or floury looking bugs, often with little tail and woolly egg masses. See Sixth: Traps, Ninth: Buying in biological controls, Tenth: Direct action, as for scale.

Thrips, sciarids and compost gnats – Little jumpy things on your sowing, potting or garden composts that resemble thunder flies. See Sixth: Traps, Ninth: Buying in biological controls, Tenth: Direct action.

Below: If it gets this bad, use scissors...

Beetles on lilies, asparagus and so on – They, or more likely their grubs, are evident, looking like tiny caterpillars or, with lily beetles, like bird droppings, and usually the leaves disappear. See Fourth: Barriers, Fifth: Hide and seek, Sixth: Traps, Seventh: Encourage natural predators, Eighth: Companion plants, Ninth: Buying in biological controls, Tenth: Direct action.

Eelworms/nematodes – Appear on potatoes as tiny sand-like cysts on the roots, otherwise the soil just seems sick of a plant, usually a crop or flower that's been there before too often. See Seventh: Encourage natural predators, Eighth: Companion plants, Ninth:Buying in biological controls, Tenth: Direct action.

Whitefly – This is an indoor infestation of tiny white flies. See Sixth: Traps, Ninth: Buying in biological controls, Tenth: Direct action.

Whitefly outdoors – Visible on brassicas, they are not the same at all as the ones found indoors, though look very similar, but they are, in fact, a wee moth. See Fourth: Barriers, Fifth: Hide and seek, Sixth: Traps, Tenth: Direct action.

Red spider mites – Usually found indoors, the leaves and shoots get tiny pinpricks, cobwebbing in bad cases and, with a lens, myriad tiny bugs are evident. See First: Healthy plants, Sixth: Traps, Ninth: Buying in biological controls, Tenth: Direct action.

Children – not yours of course, but other people's. No end of accidental damage as well as deliberate pilfering may be caused. Ensure gates are shut, and even lock them; make sure hedges and fences are secure and unclimbable, and any enticing fruit is not easily seem from the footpath.

Right: Lay such traps and inspect regularly

Diseases

Coral spot – Tiny pink, red or orange spots appear on dead wood moving onto live; simply prune and burn. See First: Healthy plants.

Clubroot – Affects the brassica family, which includes wallflowers and stocks. The roots swell, have foul-smelling content and plants fail. There is no cure, though liming heavily reduces incidence. See Second: Resistant varieties.

Honey fungus – Shrubs and trees, especially in the rose family, die, bark peels low down revealing blackish boot lace-like fungal 'roots'. This has no cure.

Mildews – Whitish, greyish or powdery deposits on leaves and fruits –see below.

Rusts – rust-coloured powdery or fluffy mouldy spots – see below.

Grey mould botrytis – grey fluffy mould, spreads like wildfire – see below.

All these diseases are treated much the same, especially with the hygienic removal of all suspect material. See First: Healthy plants, Second: Resistant varieties, Third: Cunning cultural methods, Fourth: Barriers, Eighth: Companion plants, Tenth: Direct action.

Various viruses – Leaves are mottled and yellowed, new growth is reduced and distorted, fruits misshapen and cropping poor; plant is usually best burnt. See second: Resistant varieties

Chlorosis – The leaves are mottled yellow, but symmetrically, with veins appearing greener. This is caused by a mineral deficiency and is often rectified by leaf-mould, muck or compost mulches and seaweed sprays on tops.

Wilts of seedlings – That's it exactly, they wilt then die. It's too late to do anything, but use clean water and new sowing compost next time. See First: Healthy plants, Second: Resistant varieties.

Top left: Mould is worst in stagnant conditions
Bottom left: Sooty mould like this indicates a pest problem
Right: Coral spot must be cut out before it spreads further

Your ten lines of defence

These are ten main ways in which we control pests and diseases. Each approach has different advantages and disadvantages. Some are free, others cost; there may be some effort involved or some ecological intrusion. Not all methods work for all problems, and there are some that are quite unique. Little works entirely well on its own; employing as many approaches as possible moves the balance more in our favour. Nets stop birds, but give them something else to eat or drink as well and there aren't so many trying. We also need to rely on more active methods when we come indoors, as the conditions are so different. Whereas, outdoors, we can rely on the background to provide myriad insects and other natural controls, when we come under cover we have to do more ourselves. And the warm protected conditions also mean the problems escalate more rapidly than outdoors. Fortunately, in recent years the introduction of natural biological controls for the commonest pests has made greenhouse management easy, if expensive.

Left: Seed racks from the garden shop get a second life keeping cats and birds off the seedbed

First line of defence: Healthy plants

Healthy plants rarely suffer from pests or diseases as frequently or as badly as undernourished or stressed plants. This is particularly true in the case of aphids, which do not suck sap but puncture cell walls and allow sap to be pushed through them. They extract the minerals and proteins but let the sugary bit through, which comes out the back to fall on leaves and turns them black with honeydew fungus. Aphids thus prefer higher sap pressure, which they find in plants under stress. Vigorous healthy plants can endure more damage than weak ones and also recover more quickly, therefore it reduces the need for other controls if you choose plants suitable to your soil and site, and that are growing in season. (No plants are as resilient outside their preferred timing, the earlier or later you try and make them perform, the harder it gets for them and the more they become prey to pests or disease. Plants under cover in winter suffer aphid and grey mould attacks far worse than those during the growing season.)

Water stress is, without much doubt, the worst problem after a lack of warmth for stressing plants. If they are short of water, or waterlogged, you can be sure that they will soon have pests and diseases damaging them. Good watering controls many other problems that then go by unseen.

An imbalance between water at the roots and humidity in the air causes a plethora of problems, from aphid attacks to most of the rusts, moulds and mildews. If the soil is dry and the air damp, mildews will attack especially, grapes, roses and gooseberries. In drier conditions following a long wet period they would escape. If the plants are short of water, the dew in the morning is often sufficient to enable these fungal problems to 'germinate'. Even a sagging gutter with a pool of water can initiate mildew attacks on vines nearby. But if the plant has plenty of water to call on, it's better able to resist such fungal attacks. In particular,

Right: Well watered, well fed, well weeded, well spaced and all will be well!

water stress frequently causes tomato plants, when they are confined to a bag or pot, to suffer blossom end rot, a corky brown patch on the bottom of the fruits. (Actually, this is more a mechanical problem and down to calcium shortage rather than a disease, but it will doubtless still be encountered.)

Well-balanced nutrients are similarly important, as any nutritional stress will soon allow some pest or disease to sneak in. Over-feeding makes plants more susceptible to both, as lush soft growth with over-plumped up cells is easy prey. True, starved plants are worse, but do not over-feed – it is seriously counter-productive. However, you may apply seaweed products liberally as these contain the whole spectrum of elements with none likely to overwhelm. The solution should be diluted and sprayed on and trials have shown that plants so treated have significantly less pest and disease problems. In effect, it's like us taking a multi-vitamin tablet; it does no harm in moderation and could make a big difference. Wood ashes are another important source of resistance and most plants (not the acid lovers, who find them too alkaline) are healthier given wood ashes in spring. Gooseberries and culinary apples need them the most, followed jointly by tomatoes, potatoes, onions, beetroot and most fruits.

To give plants the soil minerals in a form they can absorb, you need a plethora of soil micro-life that are sustained by the water and nutrients that are all held in the soil's humus or peaty bit. This proves the value of adding material such as well-rotted manure, leaf-mould and compost, which all feed the plants but also provide a habitat for the micro-life that also then feeds the plants. Well-rotted manure and composts are also sources of fungi that predate nematodes and other soil pests.

A balanced air flow over plants is crucial: too much and they stop transpiring (only a light wind is sufficient to reduce their growth), but stagnant air is much worse, it slows growth as it runs out of carbon dioxide and makes plants much more prone to all sorts of moulds and mildews. Damp stagnant air in low light conditions under cover makes most plants prone to grey mould and kills more of them than a colder but drier period.

Left: Annual dressing of a mix of wood ashes, lime and bone meal suits this apricot

A shortage of light makes plants less vigorous and less able to defend themselves; admittedly, too much light can scorch, but that's rarely a problem. As well as growing plants in season, make sure that all sources of shade are kept to a minimum – trees have the habit of getting taller, as do hedges! Clean all plastic and glass thoroughly in greenhouses, conservatories and cold frames and paint dark walls with white paint.

Undoubtedly, the simplest way to give a plant more of everything is to grow less of them in the same area. We all tend to overplant and oversow and then under-thin our plants. Too crowded is as bad as weeds; it makes plants weak and unable to resist other problems. You really can't over-thin or overspace; fewer plants always look and do better in the same space than too many. And fruits likewise; it is sensible to thin the heaviest crops to prevent them all being small, and it would be foolish not to take away the infected, distorted, stunted, holed, damaged and imperfect. So, by disposing of these, by burning or deep burial, we get rid of this year's infection or infestation and reduce the possibility of more next year.

Above: Given plenty of all-round light this chrysanthemum makes a full head
Right: Cold was the probable cause of death, but this dead figlet is now a source of disease and needs removing

Second line
of defence:
Resistant varieties

There are usually several options for the same garden vacancy, be it ornamental or cropping. Amongst these are some that have known weaknesses that are still grown for their esteemed qualities or heavy cropping. Others, very similar, may have complete or partial resistance to one or more of their most common afflictions. However, this may be at the cost of flavour, or whatever. Still, if you lose crops or flowers because of a known problem and there are varieties less prone or immune to it, poor flavour may be a fair exchange. I grow many crops in two varieties; the known reliable cropper and the one I really want, then I'm usually satisfied.

There is, of course, resilience as well as resistance. Plants may be immune and just not suffer a disease or pest attack, throwing it off totally, or they may be resilient and succumb to the attack yet still perform adequately despite this. Often if they can just resist a little longer then a crop or blooming can be had before the problem becomes acute. All late pea crops are a race between plant, weather and mildew, so the quicker one is more likely to succeed. Most glossy leaved roses remain freer for longer from mildew and black spot, putting on a cleaner show. Of course, you have to read the small print – seed firms may claim spurious advantages, claiming their plants are immune to diseases they never commonly suffer from, at least not when grown privately. It is not sensible to pay much more for seed that is resistant to a problem you're unlikely to experience. However, there are some good choices available, such as parsnips resistant to canker, lettuces to root aphids, carrots to their root fly, rust-resilient leeks, scab-free apples, and blight-resistant tomatoes and potatoes. Most important are clubroot-resistant brassicas; this fungal rot lives in the soil for decades and is hard to deal with any other way. Recent introductions claim full or partial resistance for some cabbages, cauliflowers and kales.

Left: There are more reliable choices, and often tastier unreliable ones

Some plant varieties have been developed to be less attractive to the pests; in particular are a whole range of carrots that do not attract the root fly by having less carroty smelling foliage. Oddly coloured varieties, or those with unusually shaped leaves, may also escape attention from pests – red versions especially so, probably as they are less easily recognised.

Growing alternative plants or crops is another way to avoid a common problem. With so many tomatoes and their close relations, potatoes, grown, there are many pests and diseases that are associated with them. *Physalis ixocarpa* is grown and fruits remarkably like a tomato for culinary use, yet it suffers very few of the problems that befall tomatoes. Celeriac is easier to grow than celery, it is more robust and is much the same for culinary use or grated for salad, but it does not suffer similar slug damage. Kohlrabi for coleslaw is far easier than cabbage, has much the same nutritional value and suffers less from most of the problems that cabbage experiences.

Rare, or uncommon, is good; as previously mentioned, if you grow the unusual, then there are seldom many pests or diseases to bother them. Most ornamentals, other than the rose family, are not related to many other ornamentals, so there are few widespread problems (other than the usual suspects, such as slugs and snails, birds, etc.). Some crop plants are also less common and so seldom suffer from pest or disease problems; these are sea kale, rhubarb, Jerusalem and Chinese and globe artichokes, sunflowers, sweet corn, salsify, scorzonera and most of the aromatic herbs. If you exclude bird and wasp damage, then some fruits are effectively pest and disease free, such as figs, mulberries, jostaberries, cranberries, blueberries, kiwis, aronia and more.

Right: Celeriac is easier to grow than celery and suffers less problems

Third line of defence: Cunning cultural methods

We have some choice as to how we grow our plants within certain bounds; at one extreme or the other, some pests or diseases may be aided or disadvantaged. We have already discussed how water stress promotes many fungal problems, whilst conversely, wet conditions are famous for slugs and snails. If we keep seedbeds wet we discourage flea beetle, which makes many small holes in seedling leaves, especially of brassica crops. Of course, in so doing we make it easier for the slugs. It depends on your priorities and other factors. Loose dusty soils may handicap many of the small weevils that bother peas and bean, and regular hoeing for weed control also disrupts ground-dwelling pests near the surface, such as leatherjackets, cut worms and slugs.

In the vegetable garden, rotating the position of crops each year is useful in two main ways: the plants are more vigorous when they grow on soil that has not seen them for several years; and there should also be few specific pests or diseases waiting for them. Certainly, the converse of not rotating is a rapid build-up of pests and diseases; in particular, it is extremely foolish to not rotate potatoes because of their nematode infections, carrots because of their root fly and brassicas because of clubroot. On the other hand, some crops, such as sweet corn, runner and broad beans may, though should not, be grown in the same spot every year with few problems if well fed. Most importantly, roses and fruit trees must be replaced by something else when they reach the end of their useful life, and it is sensible to do the same for all other plants.

Never use dirty water for sowing or for small seedlings, or for cucumber and marrow family plants, as these frequently suffer from water-borne diseases. Do not spread diseases or pests via your tools, wheelbarrow or feet. Many soil-borne problems come into your garden that

Right: Only clean water is really safe for sowing and seedlings, once they're this size, almost any water will do

way. Likewise, sterilise your secateurs, knife and saw with neat alcohol between plants. Put new plants into quarantine for a while before putting them with the rest and inspect all root-balls for vine weevil grubs and all tops for aphids and scale insects.

The early removal of a problem before it has multiplied always makes sense. Regular observation of your charges soon reveals incipient problems which may be nipped in the bud when other tasks are performed. When pruning, scale insects can be rubbed off or aphid-infested shoots trimmed away, and all obviously infected and infested material burnt or composted, especially wood with the pretty, but nasty, coral spot infection. When picking fruits or thinning, be sure to remove and burn or deeply bury all infested ones, including the chats already fallen.

With many woody plants prone to aphids you can thin the numbers overwintering by tip removal, as the insects tend to cluster there. This must not be done with those shrubs or fruits that only flower or crop on their tips, of course.

A pre-winter clean and tidy is important before moving plants to winter under cover, and check each over as it comes inside. A periodic thorough tidying and cleansing of your greenhouse, propagator and cold frame is also sensible. Likewise, in the open garden, get rid of any plant or material as soon as it is no longer needed so it cannot harbour problems over winter. And never, ever use the same strings for support year after year, as they are likely to carry over many problems, though canes can be left out to weather clean.

The use of timing can be a cunning method of defence. This can be simply by moving the crop, usually earlier than normal, to avoid the worst of a problem. Early potato varieties crop quickly, and so if also planted early they usually avoid blight. Onion sets swell and make tougher plants than plants grown from onion seed and so better resist the fly when it arrives. If you avoid touching or sowing carrots when cow parsley is flowering, you avoid the early peak of carrot root flies which are visiting native umbellifer plants. Broad beans sown in autumn and overwintered are too tough for the aphids when they arrive, and autumn-fruiting raspberries usually evade the maggots that may plague the summer croppers.

Right: Scale is hard to spot and when rubbed off often exposes a multitude of eggs

Fourth line of defence: Barriers

Although some gardeners do not like the look of nets, fleece, plastic bottle cloches and pea guards in their garden, it must be admitted that these are effective. Indeed, they are so effective it's why they have multiplied so much recently. By putting an impenetrable barrier between the problem and the plant, we defuse the situation. Blackbirds are efficiently excluded from the fruit, root flies from the carrots, and wood pigeons from brassicas by nets, fleeces and wire guards. Barriers work, and they work 24 hours a day with little attention (though, to be fair, birds do have the knack of finding any hole in a fruit cage and need evicting. Still, at least only one or two find their way in, without the cage there'd be flocks of them munching away). Barriers may be visually intrusive but they are not ecologically damaging, even any impact of their manufacture is minimised, as many gardeners recycle secondhand materials. Indeed, old net curtains do remarkably well and last longer than the proper stuff, and who has not made a cloche from a plastic bottle? In response to those who detest such 'home-made' articles, may I point out that most things can be made neat or not: a row of plastic bottles may look good or bad depending on whether they are clean, matching and tidy, or a scruffy mix of shapes, dirty and with labels flapping. But back to the point: barriers are effective. You put them in place in time and a problem is eliminated or at least significantly decreased. Perhaps, other than aesthetics, the only drawback is the storage space required for them when not in use.

Some may already use aluminium or plastic, even wooden, edging to their beds and borders. Usually employed for neatness, to retain the turf or soil and stop weeds encroaching, these also have a significant effect on small pests. Imagine a slug, snail, vine weevil or mouse trying to move from its daytime shelter to go feed on your vegetable bed, then it encounters a shiny, smooth, vertical wall it has to negotiate, and while so doing it stands out and is easy prey for any passing predator. This is especially true on its return when it has to scale this wall, as it may even become trapped in the open. Of course, there is a downside. Such a barrier

Right: Fleece is not beautiful but it efficiently keeps off weather and pests

Above left: Plastic bottle tubes prevent most ground dwellers getting to the plants
Above right: Don't wait for the damage to start before protecting trunks

does create small holes and niches behind it in the soil in which slugs and other pests can lurk during the day but, on the whole, neat continuous edging can reduce many pest attacks. Old bricks, tiles, bottles, bits of wood, or whatever, are often counter-productive though, and foster more pests than they deter.

Gardeners with raised beds with solid sides, effectively wee mountains for the pests to scale, can reinforce their isolation by fixing extra barriers to the edging, such as copper tape or sticky non-setting glue gel. The same can be run around the edge of saucers, pots, benches and their legs to stop pests moving around. Non-setting sticky bands are especially useful for banding the trunks of trees and shrubs on single stems (do not forget to also do the stake or support), thus preventing crawling pests climbing up to the foliage. This is remarkably effective against the many pests that do so climb, and allows their predators to fly in. (To stop the material soaking into the bark, first apply a ring of foil or plastic. This on its own, if wide enough, can make a slippery surface that will stop other pests climbing up, such as mice and rats.)

Fencing is often considered more for dissuading two-legged rats, but good fencing, buried into the ground and of sufficient height, stops many different creatures. Rabbits are troublesome; they will sneak under a gate, so make this fit well. Do attach a plank running up and over from the inside so if any bunnies get in they can run out again, as a trapped one eats far more! To stop deer, a fence needs to be seriously high, at head height and higher still if heavy snow is likely. Fences discourage but do not stop foxes or badgers though, who can climb or tear their way in; electric fences (as for stock) may work better in such situations.

Tree guards are wind-around plastic coils, wire netting or corrugated plastic tubes which enclose the trunk and stop rabbits nibbling the bark. (If snow falls, bunnies may be elevated and cause damage above such guards.) They're worth fitting in addition to fencing in case of the odd intrusion.

Cloches and greenhouses are usually employed as ways of improving the microclimate and excluding bad weather, however, these are also effective barriers to many pests and diseases. Of course, others may proliferate inside where the natural controls cannot get at them but, on the whole, cloches etc., are a real boon and exclude many problems. You may also need to fit netting over doors, windows and ventilators, to keep out birds, flies and butterflies.

Instead of a plastic sheet, a fine fleece, mesh or net can be used as a tent or tunnel to exclude flying and crawling pests from crops in the vegetable garden. This provides some benefit to the microclimate, but pollinators are also excluded which may be a problem for crops such as strawberries. However, these barriers stop birds, cabbage butterflies, carrot root flies, and a host of other pests from reaching our fruits and vegetables. The material may be on a frame, supported on sticks or just laid over the crop – but in this last case the pest may lay eggs through the barrier or even eat through it. (I have seen blackbirds demolish my cherries through the nylon stockings pulled over the branches to cover them.)

Many crawling pests are reluctant to scale the sides of a ring of plastic cut from a bottle or similar. The slippery shiny plastic is hard to climb so, usually, they avoid it and go elsewhere. The most ingenious I've seen were rings cut from aluminium drinks containers with the top edge consisting of myriad sharp points made by cutting with dressmaker's pinking shears – what slug or snail would climb over that?

Whereas rings cut from plastic bottles and mini-cloches made from bottles with the bottom cut off are frequently employed, tubes made from plastic bottles are less often seen. However, these are more useful than either of the former two. The tubes, made, say, from drinks bottles,

Above: Fleece or fine net physically excludes most pests
Right: Copper rings can protect vulnerable plants from ground crawlers

are approximately two to three times deeper than their width. Placed over sowings or small plants, these give a huge boost to the microclimate by keeping off the cooling winds and reducing rain and hail damage (when it's not vertical much less enters). But they also stop most crawling problems and, being deep, keep birds off too. Most importantly, being open they do not cause much of a check when removed, or can even be left in place whilst the crop matures. (For some, such as French beans, the tube will even act as a support for the heavy crop later.)

Copper rings are an expensive but most effective way of stopping slugs and snails who do not like touching copper. Copper tape is also available, which can be applied to individual pots, edges and legs. (The cleverest I've ever seen was a home-made barrier with copper wires running on top of perforated zinc separated by the insulating glue. Any slug trying to cross this actually electrocuted itself.) Do not put such an expensive ring around, say, hostas without also making sure that the leaf tips do not bend down and make a safe bridge over it.

Irritant rings are especially useful for seedlings and new transplants. They can be made from cocoa shell, wood ashes, soot, holly leaves, baked crushed eggshells, and similar, and all of which discourage slugs and other ground crawlers from approaching. These are usually less effective in wet weather and need regular topping up. A similar but thicker ring of wood ashes or soot around the trunks of gooseberries stops the sawfly caterpillars climbing back up after they have leapt off in alarm (just shake or jar the bush and they drop off).

Cardboard squares and pieces of materials such as heavy gauge, supple plastic sheet can be used to prevent pest attacks. Cut a slit from one edge to a small central hole which is fitted close around the stem of newly planted brassicas and they will prevent cabbage root flies laying their eggs in the soil close by the stem. Thus, they are forced to go elsewhere. The same can be used to keep away vine weevils.

Plastic sheets and carpet make an effective barrier to pests. Many pests overwinter under the plant they attack, and particularly troublesome are those like pear midge and gooseberry sawfly.

Left: If the pot is isolated from the saucer by the moat of water, it excludes walking pests but there must be no dry way across

By placing a barrier on top of the soil they can be trapped underneath and, unable to emerge, they die and, instead, turn to fertility. Ideally, use tightly woven or dense, fleecy, groundcover fabrics which let through air and water; plain impermeable plastic sheet works, but if it is of any size it may cause dryness and aeration problems. Economical gardeners may use carpet, upside down, though be sure to use ones that do not have moth proofer on them. The same method can reduce the numbers of pests emerging from soil or lawns such as click beetle, cranefly, cut worm and cockchafer. However, if carpet is left down long it may damage the sward – no more than three days in summer or a week in winter is fine. (See Sixth: Traps, page 66).

Vine weevil and ant moats stop these troublesome pests, especially on patios and under cover. Stand pots and containers on feet in saucers of water, or in double saucers with water between them, then the pests cannot crawl on board. Floating oil (frying, not mineral, please) on the water makes this even more effective. The legs of garden furniture, such as tables and benches, can be similarly protected. Some claim talcum powder is as effective as a moat of water, but hardly as easy to maintain.

Wire baskets, pea guards, wire netting and wire trays (recycled from cookers and fridges and bent into an arc) are ugly but very effective ways of stopping birds and cats robbing crops and messing up seedbeds. They are most needed when the crops are small and may be removed once the plants are away. Admittedly, these can be cringe-making junk, but they are singularly effective.

Horticulturally, the term cages is always combined with fruit though could also be of benefit to vegetables. Fruit cages are essential: true, netting or, better still, netting bags, tied tight about the base of a bush or tree work nearly as well, but a proper cage is better for access and air flow. The roof should be removable in case of heavy snow (and plastic net will last longer if only in place during the cropping season). The roof can be made from plastic mesh, as can the upper sides, but from knee level down use galvanised chicken netting as it is at ground level that most holes are made. The netting should be set into the ground or fixed to gravel boards which are themselves set in securely. Be sure the door is a good fit or birds will get in and will

Right: Metal grill protects peas most effectively

have to be evicted. A secondhand polytunnel makes a superb fruit cage frame and gives much more space for your money than commercial fruit cages. Use small gauge mesh, as if a bird can get its head through the body will follow. It is possible to construct cages for other crops – brassicas plagued by birds and butterflies are obvious beneficiaries, though obviously they require a finer mesh.

Polythene sheets can keep a peach or nectarine tree dry from midwinter until blossoming, thus preventing the dreaded peach leaf curl disease getting a hold, as it strikes when the buds get damp on opening. Although difficult to keep in place in windy areas, such a covering also protects the blossoms from frost, but it must be open underneath to allow pollinators access. On walls a frame can be made to fit, but be sure to leave at least the ends open for the pollinators or remove the cover every sunny day.

Dead chest freezers or refrigerators make a (metal-clad) rodent-proof store in which you can keep harvested potatoes and apples, seeds, or whatever, while confident that most pests cannot gain access and damage them. As they are insulated, they also store crops far better for longer than most other simple storage solutions. Always put seeds in something secure first, be it a plastic, metal, or preferably wooden, box. Keep this in a cool dry place, and the seeds will keep longer still if they are given a silica gel bag to absorb any moisture.

Psychological barriers have so far only been found to work with birds and bigger creatures, and although not tangible they are often as effective as a physical barrier. Doubtless, given research, we may find equivalent ploys for discouraging insects; for example, many parasites and some other insects are careful not to lay their eggs where others are already, so perhaps packets of effigy eggs could be placed by us to discourage the real ones. And maybe bottled scent of hoverfly, ladybird or lacewing larvae or whatever may deter aphids from coming to our plants. Still, we await...

Bird scarers really work, though scarecrows seldom do, as garden birds get used to people and are no longer frightened. Commercially, hawks, repeated loud bangs from compressed air guns,

Left: At last a use for it

and recordings of bird alarm calls are employed but these are not really suitable for the average garden. But birds are paranoid and jumpy and any noise, flash or movement that's sudden will make most fly off immediately. Glitter-bangs of stiff foil, or tin lids, recycled Christmas decorations and discarded CDs all work for a day or two, then the birds are habituated and ignore them. So scarers should not be left in place for weeks but moved at least every day. British birds have not read the textbooks and don't know we have no bird-eating spiders so they are easily dissuaded by the sight of a big, fat, hairy spider, or just its web. Plastic ones are sold for Halloween and can be collected after. Home-made effigies of spiders work just as well. Snakes are equally loathed and can be simply made from old hosepipe that is suitably, even artistically, painted. Replica hawks, owls and cats are all effective; you can make fake but realistic sleeping cats from old fur coats. Remember, though, to move each at least daily, preferably more often. Birds are not scared of dead cats, so also bring them in if it's raining....

I no longer recommend using audio or video tape for humming lines, as the coatings wear off and may pollute, but a commercial alternative is sold. Fishing line and black cotton strung hither and thither, especially over fruit trees and bushes, discourage birds as they think they are spiders' webs. However, some birds get caught up in them so they should not be used except in dire emergencies.

For other bigger pests, as previously mentioned, an electric fence is not ineffective. Available from agricultural stores, the voltage is never enough to kill, only to shock, and it is the sight of the wire that works ever after. Thus, the wire needs to be highly visible, or be made of smelly material.

Still working on the psychological level, smelly fox repellent has been sold for a long while. Human urine, dirty socks, unwashed hair and sweaty t-shirts are all considered deterrents for various wild creatures – and they may work temporarily if the animals are not too hungry – but do you want to have these decorating your garden? It is claimed that lion, tiger and wolf droppings stop rabbits and deer hanging around (and probably infringe umpteen health and safety bylaws), so ask your local zoo (who also have huge supplies of dung for fertiliser – elephants produce a truck-load each day). Another old method is to surround the plot or plant with a sticky string tied low on sticks for bunnies, higher for deer. This was originally

very smelly and very sticky, but commercial string became meaner and lost its effect. This was because the animals were not deterred by the string initially, but by having to clean the smelly sticky stuff off its fur afterwards, thus not wishing to incur the same again. Modern deterrent string may be so meanly made there's not enough sticky nastiness for it to work.

There are also other repellents; all sorts of noxious smelling things may deter various creatures, big and small, at least temporarily, such as soap (use soap flakes or shaving soap, not washing-up detergent), aftershave, cheap perfume, garlic, chilli, sour milk, urine, etc. Incidentally, moles ignore almost anything smelly, so don't even bother.

Above: Soap suds dry and choke pests, the smell discourages
others and the dried surface hinders their movements

Fifth line of defence: Hide and seek

To find their food, most pests use smell. Firstly this is because, apparently, most insect eyes work better close up, and secondly because smells travel further. It is said that carrot root flies can smell you touching the foliage from seven miles, though whether they could fly upwind that far, I doubt. Still, the point is that most smell from a distance, use their sight to zero in then check with smell come taste. So one solution is to camouflage our plants visually and, even more effectively, by smell.

It is well noted that unusual variations of common pest-prone plants do not always suffer to the same degree – sometimes more, sometimes less. So red-, or rather purple-, coloured brassicas may escape as much damage as the usual green forms and birds are often fooled into leaving yellow ripening berries which they 'expect' to ripen red. Perhaps an edible dye might one day make certain crops 'invisible'.

Intercropping, mixing plants, to hide shape and smell does work, simply by making each harder to spot than when grown in a monoculture. (And it is also harder for an infestation or infection to spread.) It has long been common to grow onions and carrots together, as each masks the other's smell from their

'They seek them here they seek them there they seek out your crops most anywhere.'

Below: Unusual coloured crops may evade detection

flies. Likewise, when brassicas are grown with French beans, both suffer fewer attacks from several assorted pests, and lavender under roses is believed to dissuade aphids. Though we are verging on companion planting here, there is a subtle distinction, and we need to be careful; sometimes a negative companion effect, or just plain competition, can outweigh an intercropping advantage. When investigating the theory that wormwood (artemisia) exuded such a strong smell that it deterred butterflies from laying on brassicas, they discovered this to be true; but the cabbages liked the wormwood's exudations even less and their yield dropped unacceptably. So, perhaps the best policy is to have confusing smells produced around but not amongst the protected crop.

So place camouflage smells with barriers of rosemary, hyssop, southernwood or lavender as hedges around a plot to hide the scents of the vegetables. French marigolds prove efficacious at stopping white flies entering greenhouses, but will not drive them out if they are already there or when carried in on a plant. Shoofly (nicandra), is considered equally efficacious but it is too large, and poisonous. Stinging nettle tea, garlic tea, soap solution or seaweed sprays can help by similarly masking the smell of plants, as well as giving some boost to health and vigour.

Fleece can be very effective, not as a barrier but for hide and seek. Two-legged rats steal from allotments and back gardens, they are in a hurry and take what they see so most will never take time to investigate that which is hidden.

Sacrificial crops are grown to be taken in place of the main crop, so usually they are positioned on the perimeter of the bed. They may be the same as the crop, or ideally a preferable plant. Chinese cabbage will lure slugs away from ordinary lettuce or cabbage; the variety Buffalo is more slug-palatable than most autumn-sown onions and can be mixed with them to take most injury itself and so save the crop. Extra grapevines run over trees lure away the birds, as can raspberries grown next to the strawberry bed.

Right: A herbal scented barrier may deter many pests

Sixth line of defence: Traps

You can simply reduce pest numbers by trapping them, sometimes preventing scouts bringing more. Obviously more traps work better than one, with some you need dozens to have an effect. The right bait in the right place means there is a learning curve as to which will be most effective. You do not want by-catch – other things being trapped instead of the intended victims – so be careful again with bait and where you place the trap. It is humane to visit all traps at least daily and put out of their misery those suffering slow deaths – then to the compost heap with them.

Mouse traps need no description, similar rat traps are bigger and seriously dangerous to fingers. These are useful in every area, but where birds may gain access put them in places birds will not venture, such as dark corners. Many are mechanical and kill most times, but some are glue based so the animals suffer slow death from dehydration. No-kill rodent traps are available but then they leave you with a problem: kill the animals yourself or (illegally) take them somewhere (far away) for release to cause both them and someone else trouble.

Cage traps are sold for bigger animals in various sizes. Most operate with a drop-down door and, if suitably placed and baited, they work well for rats, rabbits, wood pigeons and other big pests. But, depending on the bait you use, they may also trap hedgehogs and cats. Regular inspections are legally necessary, as well as humane. Once caught, you again have the disposal problem.

Mole traps are, as far as I've found, relatively ineffectual except for the chance catch. The mole is very sensitive to disturbance and smells and wisely avoids odd items intruding into its world (though pouring smelly stuff in their runs is usually totally ineffective). The professionals are better at the accurate setting of such traps and are worth their fee.

'This is war, and prisoners need dispatching, can you do it?'

Above left: A cage trap catches without any harm
Above right: A mole trap usually kills immediately

Slug pubs are very effective. Slugs are especially attracted to wilting foliage and fermenting fruits, so they will search out saucers or lids of fermenting orange juice, beer or even milk and obligingly drown themselves. If these pubs are set level into the ground, even better. Unfortunately, the very useful ground beetles also drop in for a drink and drown, too, so put in some bushy twigs to help the beetles get out – who (sorry for this) never get as legless as the slugs.

Wasps search out jammy water in jam jars or bottles hung amongst ripening fruit. These traps work best when covered with a foil lid perforated by a sharp pencil from the top to make wee pencil-size holes with inward protruding teeth. The wasps climb in but can't easily climb out, fall into the water and drown. The disgusting result is valuable poured on the compost. These also catch flies and some other insects. Never use honey or you will trap bees too.

Fly bottles are similar to wasp traps, being simply bottles laid on their sides that are full to overflowing with jammy water. The insects get in but find it hard to leave.

Stacks of saucers and plates, tiles, or bricks hidden in damp shady places and under evergreens and so on attract slugs and New Zealand flatworms, which can be cleared out with, say, fornightly inspections. Likewise, stacks of bottles are a magnet to snails. Lodge these neck-down so they don't collect water and act as deadfall traps to all and sundry.

Fly papers are another old, simple solution and are very effective if hung in sufficient numbers. They are also useful in other ways; wrapped about a piece of card and waved over flea beetles (which make small holes in brassica seedlings), which will jump up when disturbed and stick. Or wind fly paper around the trunk of a tree (ideally on top of a polythene wrap) and you will trap ants and other bugs on their way for lunch. Likewise, a piece of stiff board coated with treacle or golden syrup will catch crawling pests if placed under or around plants. You can buy yellow sticky traps as this colour attracts several pests – though these are sold as indicators, not as effective traps. Sticky sheets laid under potted plants are good for trapping thrips and other pests that drop down when disturbed, such as vine weevils, and most sawfly and moth caterpillars.

Making a hole to insert a slug pub /old aerosol cap

Setting cap almost flush with soil

Adding attractant- fermenting fruit juice

A few sticks help less legless beetles clamber out

Pheromone traps are sticky traps baited with the pest's sex hormone, so the males come flying after some tasty female scent, only to arrive to find a sticky end. They are again useful as indicators of an attack under way so that other methods can be deployed.

A fly paper or a ring of non-setting glue about a trunk will act as a barrier to some pests, as mentioned before, while doubtless many others get caught. Because of this, and dust, sticky bands need regular topping up. Ants, in particular, cunningly bridge such traps, with their own kind if necessary, so again regular replenishment helps. Also, multiple rings are more effective than one. Non-setting compounds should not be painted onto the trunk but onto a protective wrap of polythene or foil.

Cloth and cardboard bands can go above and below a sticky band, then the pests, when thwarted in their travels, hide up in these close copies of loose rough bark. Unfortunately, so do some friendly critters. So, on inspection, take care to save the ladybirds and lacewings before dropping the assorted moth and bug eggs, larvae and adults into a bucket of soapy water, then onto the compost with them.

Tubes and nooks, such as bits of bamboo, narrow cardboard tubes, rolls of corrugated cardboard and pots stuffed with straw, attract earwigs who hide there to be evicted and drowned. These are especially effective stuck on sticks above infested plants. Likewise, vine weevil most like the gap that forms between the soil and wall, as do several other critters, some friendly. So, knowing they are there, on a dry day you should vacuum them all out and sort the spoil. Wood off-cuts of, say, paperback-book size but thinner, moistened, soiled and stacked amongst potted plants or by the base of staging, can lure in woodlice and millipedes. Have a vacuum cleaner running when you dismantle each stack as they are hard to collect by hand. They can go on the bird table in a bowl stood in a big saucer of water so they don't just run away.

Left: Watering then laying old carpet
brings up many pests for the birds

Really soak a bed, lawn or whatever area you want cleared, then lay down carpet, groundcover fabric or an opaque plastic sheet. Leave it for a few days on grass, longer on soil and the click beetle larvae, leather jacket cranefly larvae, slugs and snails will come to enjoy the surface feast. Roll the cover away early one morning and all will be caught napping, then let the wild birds, or hens if you have them, do the slaughter.

Hot pots are a good solution to ant infestations. Place several tins or pots inverted on the ground in summer where you know there are ants' nests, and ants will bring their 'eggs' or cocoons into them. After a week or so, on a sunny afternoon, lift away the pot with its contents using a trowel to scrape up any escaping soil and eggs. These can be given to fish or hens or wild birds, as they come mixed with the dirt. (To get clean eggs, spread the soil, ants and eggs on an empty tray sitting in a bigger tray of water. Place a tin lid on the soil propped up a crack by a tiny stone and shade this with a big leaf. The ants will find they cannot escape or dig down so they will neatly place all the egg cocoons in the safest place – under the lid for you to collect. Neat, hey?)

Some of the surplus and the waste we are sending to the compost can first act as a trap for pests such as slugs, woodlice and millipedes. Orange skins, hollowed out half marrows, half spuds, parsnips, and other roots and apples all work. How could they refuse the inviting, damp, shaded, food-filled hollow placed against the soil? Regular inspection and eviction will soon thin out the pests. One cure I like, but I'm not sure works that well, is the use of piles of oat or wheat bran to lure slugs which, when they eat it dry, causes them to burst. Certainly these and any germinating grains are good baits to put in other traps for insect grubs, or for spreading before laying down a plastic or carpet sheet, as mentioned above. Bran and grain are also very attractive to millipedes and wireworms.

Right: It's all happening at night – go out with a torch

Bait plants are plants that are even more attractive to pests than the crop and are another form of sacrificial plant (see page 64), but the difference being that we grow these to be discarded, carrying the pest with them. They're very useful undercover where we have little help from the natural systems. Broad beans are very good for luring red spider mite onto them, tobacco plants for attracting whitefly, and tomatoes and potatoes (use spare tubers with sprouts on) for mealy bugs. Place these bait plants intimately with the infested plants and, after a week or so, carefully remove them and burn or compost them. (Spray the tobacco plants with sugar syrup – or even hair spray – before moving them to stop the whitefly fleeing.)

In the open ground, a planting of *Solanum sisymbriifolium* awakens the cysts of the potato root knot nematodes which can ruin yields. However, although it awakens them it does not sustain them, so they die out. Then a potato crop can be grown there the following year, which would never have succeeded otherwise. Mustard can be used in the same way to decrease clubroot disease. It is sown thickly, awakens the spores, but is then dug in or removed before they can feed. Six months to a year later the same method is repeated. After several treatments the infestation is reduced. Some other trap plants are, likewise, thought to clear the soils of certain pests and diseases. Soya beans clear root rots before a strawberry crop and scab before potatoes. Marigolds – French and African – are good at clearing many pernicious nematodes, but the best is the giant Mexican *Tagetes minuta*. All this is companion planting again in another guise – see Eighth line of defence: Companion plants (page 86).

'If we can't outsmart the pests we do not deserve to succeed.'

Left: Sarracenia plants are amazingly effective at keeping down flies

Seventh line of defence: Encourage natural predators

These are how nature prevents any one creature from swamping out everything else. Not only are there predators that hunt down, kill and eat (usually in that order, but not always) prey themselves, there are others who catch prey as a larder for their offspring which then live off their bodies, sometimes still alive but paralysed. Then there are parasites who use others as a larder whilst still alive, usually fatally. Generally all these are quick movers, big and small; they have to be to catch their prey. There are, of course, also diseases to control populations and though these are harder to encourage, some can be bought in (see Ninth: Buying in biological controls, page 94).

There are also fungi that control nematodes and eelworms, some physically trap them, others work by invasion, and there are countless other pathogens and exudations for almost every soil organism – general and specific. Garden compost can also be effective as it is full of myriad forms of life and, when it is applied to soil, it wages an invisible war. The controls are automatic; as soon as anything is in any number it becomes a food resource for something else, which increases in proportion until a balance is reached. Also, soil fed with compost is of a better texture and colour, is water stable with an increased water-holding capacity, and is rich in diverse nutrients. All of which makes for healthier plants that are well able to resist pests and diseases. Some have found that extracts of compost work almost as well as large applications, these can be watered onto the soil or potting compost or even applied as a foliar feed. (Fill an old pair of tights with compost and drop this in the water butt to infuse the water. Replace it with a fresh load after about a month.)

Right: Compost ensures soil health, as well as fertility

Don't use nasty sprays on pests – unfortunately, most pesticides and many herbicides kill all sorts of other creatures as well as their intended target. Some even leave poisonous residues, to say nothing about the factory making them. Although, in desperation, some might use them, I prefer to find an alternative or to use the least generally toxic versions. Many powders and sprays that were once thought benign are now known to be too harmful or too risky to use, and their legal position also changes in different countries. So greener gardeners are no longer applying even plant-based products such as tobacco, quassia, derris and pyrethrum, even if these may still be available. Although most modern sprays are better researched and more specific to the pest they are killing, they should still be spurned because of the unknown long-term implications.

Provide water, food, warmth and winter homes for beneficial creatures. Water is most crucial, so provide a multitude of choice for all sizes of animals and insects, from a fountain, pool, bird bath and in the leaves and joints of good companions such as *Alchemilla mollis*, lupins and teasels, and keep the soil moist and well mulched. Food is best provided by diverse plants giving nectar and pollen to the adult insects, in order to lay better eggs in larger quantities. Warmth is essential as the warmer it is the more nectar flows and the more insects roam. Improve warmth with shelter, hedges, thick shrubby corners and piles of rocks in sunny spots. It's not exactly pretty, but sheets of old tin are useful to attract snakes to bask underneath. But most important is not to be too tidy; try to leave some natural debris of sticks and dead leaves, even dead wood, and make all sorts of hibernating and nesting places with boxes for the birds, hedgehog dens, toad pots in damp cool places, and piles of rotting wood for wasps to recycle for their papery nests as, although a pest on fruit, wasps are also useful pest controllers themselves. Ladybird hostels and lacewing hotels of hollow stems and bamboo sections bundled together and hidden in dry places, such as inside evergreens, are slow to be found but will then be used for many years.

Top left: A bit small even for a robin but worth a try
Bottom left: A bit more hopeful and would suit a tit
Top right: Is this the des. res. for a hedgehog?
Bottom right: Hollow stems equal hotel cabins for wee critters

In order to keep a predator population alive you need to keep feeding them with their prey; thus, sometimes you can grow banker plants that are prone to a pest, in order to provide a continuous supply of them. In this way you keep alive their predators, which will stop these or another pest on the other plants around them. Well, that's the theory, which seems to work, some of the time anyway. So we plant vetches in wilder corners to carry aphids, which apparently are best for fattening up ladybirds. Allowing the aphids free reign on the cherries and honeysuckles may mean they feed and breed enough ladybirds and other predators to keep the rest of the garden clean. And, on the bright side, all that honeydew and dead aphid skins are a tremendous boost to the fertility of the soil.

Providing more different habitats is a good way to increase the diversity of insect life in the garden and, thus, the auto-control. Have areas of long as well as short grass, areas mulched with coarse bark and others with sand. Make shady damp piles of logs or stones, and dry ones the same, and have wet boggy areas next to pools. The more different habitats you have, the better.

Left: A bird bath is a good investment

The cast of ostensible friends?

Hedgehogs – Too well known to need a description, these animals are omnivorous, eating anything they can squeeze in. So, along with a few pests, they also eat worms and a huge number of beetles. I suspect, heretically, they are, on average, counterproductive to our ends. They are cute, though, and need water, cat food and a warm box under a shed.

The mixed blessing of birds – As with hedgehogs, the damage they do is about the same as their benefit, but as they're also cute and sing, it's worth having bird boxes of all sizes and shapes, bird baths, bird tables and plenty of perches. Just think of all that potent fertiliser they're spreading around, if nothing else.

Hens and ducks – A serious natural method of pest control – I have no vine weevils where the hens run! Looking after them is beyond the scope of this book but I am serious; with careful fencing and controlled visits, a few hens eat a lot of protein for free when roaming around. Ducks are better slug and snail controllers, though, and Muscovies snap flies from the air. Handy!

Cold-blooded friends – newts, lizards, frogs, toads and slow worms all eat pests but also everything else they can catch, so these may be another mixed blessing. Still, encourage them with more damp habitats, rock piles, more pools, even small ones, and more groundcover so they can move around unmolested.

Cats – Hugely controversial animals, as some do occasionally take birds, but their control of rats, voles and mice makes them well worth having. Small well-fed females are the best hunters, neutered males are usually no more than sleeping policemen.

Top left: A hen and chicks will eat a lot of seeds and bugs
Top right: All spiders are insectivores and so friends to gardeners
Botto m left: Round and black millipedes, mostly pests, flat and brown centipede, mostly useful
Bottom right: Smokey; well camouflaged, she mugs grey squirrels

Bugs to catch bugs – As is noted, the problem with the larger predators is they don't stick to one prey and may do as much damage to our ecosystem as help. Smaller creatures are often more specific about their lunch, although there are omnivores eating everything and there are usually several controls for every pest. In general, the larvae do the control, the adults the breeding and some control. We encourage the latter with certain plants which feed a range of different insects, especially: *Convolvulus tricolor*, *Phacelia tanacetifolia*, *Limnanthes douglasii*, *Fagopyrum esculentum* (buckwheat), yarrow, and leeks, celery and carrots let go to flower.

Tolerate wasps – This is especially hard as they are so vicious, but they do consume huge numbers of pests as they are carnivorous and rarely take nectar or pollen. If you must kill the nest, leave it as late as possible so some queens may mature and escape for next year's nests. (I recommend getting in the professionals for this!)

Spiders – These are all carnivores and should be encouraged with tolerance and given small hollow stem sections to live in, and where you want their webs, tie strings first to keep them away from paths. If you have them under cover, give them bottle caps of water as they may otherwise die of dehydration.

Ground beetles – Those violet ones, the Devil's coach horses, and many others are friends, eating slugs and their eggs and many other different pest eggs. They should be encouraged with groundcover, especially long grassy areas, coarse bark mulches, rotting log piles and similar.

Wood lice, earwigs, millipedes and centipedes – The first three are, undoubtedly, also pests, but at the same time they eat other pests, too. If they are in great numbers, then use the traps listed on page 72. They are encouraged by similar conditions to those for ground beetles.

Right: Spiders are all friends and can be encouraged to make webs by placing strings or sticks in suitable places

Eighth line
of defence:
Companion plants

These are two or more different plants grown together for the benefit of one or more plant. Simple intercropping increases yields, for example: two beds both with a mixture of, say, sweet corn and French beans, and with the same total number of plants, produces more than a monocrop bed of each. We've already discussed crops grown beforehand to clear soil problems, but true companions are usually grown with the crop. They may be grown for support or shelter, or one may create root tunnels exploited by the other, but basically one helps the other, inadvertently, as in fact they are competitors. We can use good companions for attracting or repelling pests, or attracting predators and parasites to our plants. Some have been mentioned before, and there are several specific associations on the vegetable plot (see page 91).

Some plant combinations encourage more vigour in one or both when combined with another; strawberries grow well with borage, chamomile aids sick plants to recover, and stinging nettles nearby make fruit keep fresh longer.

Plants can provide micro-nutrients and antibiotics. It may well be that the various exudations plants make to get rid of waste products, dissolve soil whilst scavenging for nutrients, and to defend themselves against microbial attack, are just what the other plant needs to make it healthy. And with each exudation, leaf litter, pollen and petal fall, root hair death and decay stimulating soil micro-life, myriads more of these complex substances are liberated into the soil.

Right: Running French beans and sweet corn get on really well

Companion plants also help by aiding fertility generally or specifically; the most well known companions are the legumes, the pea and bean, lupine, laburnum, and clover family. These have nodules on their roots stuffed with nitrogen-fixing bugs that provide for the host plants and create a surplus for others. Some plants accumulate various minerals and micro-nutrients and, again, render them available to those grown with or after them. Comfrey is well known for accumulating potassium and thornapple (datura) collects phosphates.

One of the strangest companion effects is communication; it has been shown that, when plants are under attack, some give off exudations that act as warnings to others who can increase their defences ready for an attack.

It is notable that one of the oldest companion associations we know involves three plants – squashes, beans and sweet corn – which were grown together by the ancient South American natives and still do well together today. It may well be that multiple associations are the more effective, it's just we haven't worked them out yet.

There are some specific companions that are worth using. Alliums, particularly chives and garlic, when planted en masse benefit roses and fruits, making them more resistant to fungal attacks, while beds of lavender under roses reduce aphids. Growing trailing nasturtiums over the trees discourages apple woolly aphis, though it takes three years to finally drive them away. The benefits of marigolds (tagetes) for discouraging nematodes and whitefly have already been mentioned, but it is worth repeating; pot marigolds are not as effective, but they are still beneficial. Asparagus and tomatoes make good companions because their root exudations protect each other from attacks.

However, it's also important to keep bad companions apart, such as planting the beans away from the onions and other alliums, and keeping peppers away from radishes, which themselves dislike hyssop. Pears do not like grass close underneath; rue is disliked by basil, brassicas, courgettes and lettuce, and wormwood is hated by just about everything.

Right: Comfrey makes a good liquid feed and, more importantly its flowers are good for beneficial insects

Vegetable bed companionships

Some crops do better or less well when grown near others, so it's worth knowing what these combinations are.

Beans, broad and field – Do better with brassicas, carrots, celery, cucurbits, potatoes, summer savory and most herbs. They do less well with onions and garlic.

Beans, French – Do better with celery, cucurbits, potatoes, strawberries and sweet corn. Do less well with onions and garlic.

Beans, Runner – Do better with sweet corn and summer savory. Do less well with beetroot, chards, and kohlrabi.

Beetroot and chards – Do better with most beans, brassicas, onions and garlic, kohlrabi, parsnips, turnips and swedes. Do less well with runner beans.

Brassicas, cabbage family – Do better with beetroot and chards, celery, dill, nasturtiums, onions and garlic, peas and potatoes. Do less well with runner beans and strawberries.

Carrots – Do better with chives, leeks, lettuce, onions and garlic, peas and tomatoes.

Celery and celeriac – Do better with brassicas, beans, leeks and tomatoes.

Left: Carrot seedlings smell so strongly, their pests soon find them unless camouflaged with smellier companions such as spring onions

Cucurbits: cucumber, courgette, marrow, melons, pumpkin and squashes – Do better with beans, French and runner, and sweet corn. Do less well with nasturtium, peas and potatoes.

Leeks – Do better with carrots, celery and onions.

Lettuce – Does better with carrots, cucurbits, radishes, strawberries and chervil.

Onions and garlic – Do better with beetroot and chards, lettuce, strawberry, summer savory and tomatoes. Do less well with beans and peas.

Peas – Do better with beans, carrots, cucurbits, sweet corn, turnips and potatoes. Do less well with onions and garlic.

Potatoes – Do better with beans, brassicas, peas, asparagus and sweet corn. Do less well with tomatoes and cucurbits.

Sweet corn – Does better with beans, brassicas, cucurbits, peas, potatoes and sunflowers.

Sweet and chilli peppers – Do better with basil. Do less well with kohlrabi, and radishes.

Sunflowers – Do better with cucurbits and nasturtiums. Do less well with potatoes, runner beans, sweet corn and grasses.

Tomatoes – Do better with asparagus, basil, carrots, brassicas, onions and garlic and parsley. Do less well with kohlrabi and potatoes.

Turnips and Swedes – Do better with peas.

Right: Potatoes get on really well with peas

Ninth line of defence: Buying in biological controls

This is not as new as you may suspect; the first use of an encarsia wasp to control whitefly under glass was before World War I, but became impractical when insecticides came into general use. The idea is simple – there are natural predators, parasites and pathogens to prey on every creature so the most effective of these are sold commercially. They are not cheap but are incredibly straightforward – you pay, they arrive suitably packaged and you give them access to the problem. Most were initially intended for pests under cover, where they are concentrated with their prey, but others are now available for several outdoor pest and disease problems.

It is important to follow the instructions; some come as powders or mixtures with bran or whatever to be placed on the plants, others in sachets to be opened and hung, some need mixing with warm water and pouring on the soil or compost. As so many are now available, there is barely a common pest they can't deal with.

For best results, you need to get the timing right. It is little use liberating hungry predators before the pests appear, as they may starve. So, usually, controls are sent out at the usual invasion time or you order them as soon as a problem appears. You can contract for them to be timed to arrive to deal with most pests before these have even appeared in number. One company sends out mixtures of nematodes (remember some others are pests, these ones are

Right: Some controls are simply tapped out of their packaging

microscopic eelworms that prey on pests) to control carrot root fly, cabbage root fly, onion fly, sciarid fly, gooseberry sawfly, general caterpillars, leatherjackets, cutworms, ants, thrips and codling moth, all in one application, with follow-ups available later. Sometimes you may introduce the pest first, thus ensuring the control feeds and multiplies and is established before the real invasion occurs. If the pest has already multiplied, it helps to thin pest numbers by means that will not harm the control when it is introduced, such as sacrificial trap plants, sticky traps, soft soap or a vacuum cleaner.

Hyper-predation is when different controls are used and interact – one control eating another. Although this could occur, it seldom happens in practice. Even so, it's sensible to ask the vendor if different controls are best used in the same greenhouse together or at different times.

Be warned, these controls are expensive. Many of them come by mail order, but some can now be found in garden centres. It appears cheaper to buy a pack and split it with a friend, but then neither of you may have enough of the control to do a good job. It is better if you buy the bigger packs, which are also more economical, and split those. Once the pests die out, so do the predators usually, so you may have to buy again next year. This is less of a problem with the outdoor soil controls and these may continue giving some protection.

'A control in time saves nine.'

Left: Many controls are applied onto the affected plants in bran

What control to use and when

(Those marked * are predominantly for indoor use.)

Whitefly* – The control is *Encarsia formosa*, a tiny wasp simply released once the temperature of the greenhouse reaches at least 10°C (50°F).

Red spider mite* – the control is *Phytoseiulus persimilis*, a tiny mite that is simply released, though heavy infestations may need prior syringing.

Caterpillars – These are best controlled by *Bacillus thuringiensis*. Not available currently to amateurs in all countries, this is excellent for pests such as cabbage caterpillars. Spray or dust the disease-containing compound onto plants, the caterpillars eat it and then die of a disease they could contract naturally anyway.

Aphids* – These are best controlled by *Aphidoletes aphidimyza*, a parasitic midge which needs a temperature of 10°C (50°F) to thrive. Aphids can also be controlled with a minute wasp, *Aphidius*, and by ladybirds and lacewings. I find native ones in 'golden' parasitized aphids on the backs of Eglantine rose leaves in spring and take these to my greenhouse to hatch.

Thrips and sciarid or compost flies* – Use *Ambleysius* or *Hypoaspis* predatory mites outdoors when the temperature is above 11°C (52°F).

Leaf miners – *Dacnusa/Digylphus* is used commercially and may soon be available to amateurs.

Caterpillars can be controlled by a
Bacillus, where available

Scale and mealy bugs* – Under cover in temperatures above 14°C (57°F), use the parasitic nematode *Steinernema* to parasitize the scales or release a parasitic wasp *Metaphycus helvolus*. For mealy bugs, introduce *Cryptolaemus montrouzieri*, a ladybird whose shaggy white larvae work at temperatures above 11°C (52°F). Both mealy bug and scale are controlled by lacewings, and on low-growing plants by *Hypoaspis*.

Vine weevil – Water on a solution of the biological controls *Heterorhabditis megidis* or *Steinernema carpocapsae* when the soil temperature is over 12°C (54°F). The soil must be moist, as these microscopic nematodes swim in the soil moisture, searching for grubs to parasitize.

Slugs – Use *Phasmarhabditis hermaphrodita* when the soil is moist and has reached a temperature of above 5°C (41°F). Water on the nematode, repeating the application every six weeks.

Ants – Another parasitic nematode, *Steinernema feltiae*, is watered onto the ants' nest any time the soil is moist and at a temperature of above 12°C (54°F).

Chafers – These can be controlled by watering on a solution of the parasitic nematode *Heterorhabditis megidis* when the soil is wet and warmer than 12°C (54°F).

Leatherjackets – Water on *Steinernema feltiae* nematodes when the soil is wet and warmer than 10°C (50°F).

Trichoderma virides, a parasitic fungus of other fungi, has been used for Dutch Elm and Silver Leaf diseases, against wilt, and as a wound treatment, but it is not currently available to amateurs in the UK.

Left: Ants farm worse pests and must be controlled

Tenth line of defence: Direct action

When other methods are not successful, simply killing the pests yourself directly, or indirectly, even with poisons may be necessary. Likewise, some sprays or other applications may be needed to control diseases that are otherwise hard to prevent. As always, prompt, early action is important, and observation is the key, especially at night with a torch...

Hand picking and squashing pests underfoot or between finger and thumb, or dropping them into salty or boiling water, cutting them up with scissors or whatever gruesome method you choose, can be effective for bigger pests, such as cabbage caterpillars and slugs, which are easy to eradicate if you are methodical. Hairy caterpillars may need rubber gloves to be safely handled and those forming webbing nests may need the whole lot burning in one go with them aboard. However, if not pleasant to do, such actions are effective. Gooseberry sawflies all start on one leaf and can be eliminated in one fell swoop. Slugs and snails are remarkably easy to capture and dispose of, while wood lice, millipedes and other small scurrying creatures can be caught with a hand vacuum cleaner. A more powerful model can suck up all the contents of a wasps' nest as they attempt to come or go – of course, once captured you need to then dispose of the bag without them escaping, which is tricky. A simple way is to pop the bag or receptacle in a chest freezer and chill them to death. Do not be squeamish and set pests free over the fence, as they will be back. Death is the only sensible solution. Vine weevils make a particularly satisfying crunch!

For a few problems, such as aphids on roses, simply squirting them with high-pressure water will dislodge the pests and send them many yards away; from which most will never return. Obviously this approach is less effective on plants under cover, but even so, continuous harassment with a powerful jet can reduce many populations considerably, if not totally.

Right: Laugh not - a hand car vac is a good way of thinning out greenhouse whitefly or catching ants or wood lice

Steam generators work really well to sterilise or at least deep-clean pots, trays (not meltable plastic!), greenhouses and cold frames, etc. They can be hired or small ones can be bought cheaply. The steam is good for getting into cracks and places that are hard to brush clean. Although the temperature is high, it may not kill all disease organisms but will reduce their number and most pests will be near totally eliminated. (P.S. I suggest steam cleaning not pressure washing – the latter will remove the panes of glass in your greenhouse most effectively!)

Interestingly, some cheap edible substances such as sugar, starch, milk, vinegar and so on have all exhibited control of various fungal and other problems, but they can't legally be recommended. Washing-up liquid detergent is often used, quite wrongly, not only because of illegality but because it's too strong and hurts the plants. Soft soap is almost innocuous and has long been used to control pests. It dries on the pests, impeding their motion and blocking their breathing holes so smaller critters are killed while larger ones may survive. It is not very selective, though, so friends and enemies are both killed. None the less, spraying or dipping can be very effective, especially for heavy infestations. Do not apply in hot sun or strong winds, as the soap may strip protective oils from leaves, making them scorch or sear. Soft soap is not washing-up liquid, which is a strong detergent and bad for plants. The old-fashioned soap flakes for washing woollen clothes were once very successfully used at a dilution of 120ml per 4.5 litres of warm rain water, but are no longer legal as a pesticide in the UK. Still, if you are only washing plants and the pests accidentally expire... Commercial formulated soaps work even better and are sold for pest control, but follow their instructions! I found applying soft soap as foam made with a shaving brush most effective against scale and similar problems.

Spraying poisons must be the last resort; not only do most poisons kill all sorts of critters, big and small, damage the soil ecology and even the plants, but, worse, they may damage you or your children or pets. Even if used correctly, many are still risky and more so whilst concentrated, so please store even apparently safe substances where children and pets cannot get at them. There are only two things you need to know when using poisons:

Left: Painting rum, meths or surgical spirit on mealy bug dissolves their coat and sucks their life away

Rule no.1. Read the instructions (especially check you have the right product for the right target).

Rule no.2. Follow those instructions (re-read rule 1).

Organic, bio-dynamic and generally green gardeners will prefer not to use any 'chemical' poisons at all. Although some mostly 'natural' ones are or were allowed under Organic standards, few are now legally available in many countries.

Quassia, a wood extract, has long been known to kill aphids and other small pests yet it is thought safe for us and the environment. Pyrethrum, the powdered dried flowers of a chrysanthemum, has been used since ancient times and was thought safe but is now considered risky. (Some modern chemicals known as synthetic pyrethroids are based on this and may be 'safer'.) Derris, a root extract, was also thought safe but now raises doubts. Nicotine really was not safe at all, in fact it killed some gardeners inadvertently and, as tobacco, many more, however it is a very strong insecticide used as a solution or smoke.

Please remember that bees visit flowers, so never, ever spray anything risky on plants in bloom. And if you really must spray something, do so last thing in the evening when the bees have packed up for the day.

Dusts are applied most successfully with pump-action puffers; these are difficult to use outdoors, because of wind, but they work well under cover. Dusts need to coat to work and will stick best if the plants and bugs are dew-wet, such as soon after dawn. An old trick was to powder the soil under a plant and blow this on the infestation – the finer particles would clog the critters' joints and pores, possibly infecting them with a disease or nematode as well. Likewise, any fine dust will certainly make life awkward for pests and probably do them some harm. It can later be syringed off the plants. (Be aware, dusting with soil could infect plants with a soil-borne disease!). Solutions can be applied with a pressure sprayer or even a recycled household squeeze-action bottle. Outdoors, the wind causes difficulty but on still days it's possible to give a good coating. The finer the spray the better the coating, but the more the

Left: Never apply anything to plants in flower, as the bees may suffer

wind blows it about. Under cover it's easy to do a good job in situ, though it is better to move the plants to a clear spot stood on a plastic sheet, even surrounded by another sheet, to catch the drips and waste.

Foams, such as insecticidal soaps, worked up with a shaving brush and applied by hand, give good and effective coverage and are excellent for treating pests such as scale insects, woolly aphis and mealy bug on rough bark.

Although 'chemical' sprays are generally abhorrent, some fungal sprays are effective and, although chemical, are considered reasonably safe. Bordeaux mixture was originally used to discourage children stealing grapes. It is a mixture of copper sulphate in lime-wash and, although toxic in quantity, relatively safe and not particularly harmful to the environment. It is a very effective treatment for preventing fungal attacks, especially those on peaches and potatoes and currently allowed under Organic standards. The powder is puffed or sprayed on as a liquid suspension, with all proper precautions.

Sulphur dust was once administered with treacle as a health aid. This can be puffed onto grapevines to prevent mildew, at which it is singularly effective. It is also handy for preventing rots on wounds, especially bulbs and tubers.

Sodium bicarbonate is as safe as the cakes in which it's used, and every baked product and patent medicine. This innocuous powder, when made into solution and sprayed on, is remarkably effective against mildew on gooseberries and many other plants, although it is not legal in the UK.

For botrytis, grey mould, on soft fruit and salads, fresh neat urine has been sprayed with remarkable efficacy. Urine is normally sterile and seldom carries disease; it's the urea that is thought to give it the anti-fungal effect. But most find the use distasteful, and probably illegal, so not recommended.

Right: Oops, what's health and safety for Bob?

The final solution — eat your way out of the problem

A huge number of pests are edible, even if not considered palatable or even legal fare to our culture. Wood pigeons, rabbits and deer are still obviously very much a fair lunch for many. Squirrels and smaller birds are as tasty but less eaten by most of the British, whilst snails, rats and other rodents leave us aghast yet are much enjoyed elsewhere. Thanks to recent celebrity TV shows, even eating grubs of all sorts is no longer unknown, if not exactly starting a new dining trend. Most insects are also edible, if not palatable, in parts, albeit small ones. Locusts, once cooked, are not dissimilar to prawns, or grasshoppers to shrimps, and really quite good. (The Bible lists forbidden, and permitted foods, and, surprisingly, locusts and grasshoppers are amongst permissible 'meats'.) The potential is huge. Wood lice are related to lobsters and some aphids are so big (look at your lupins) you could almost barbecue them...

And sometimes there's no point worrying for, as my old gran said when I complained about seeing little maggots on a forkful of delicious home-grown peas: 'Well, don't look so hard then.'

Below: One man's poison is another man's meat

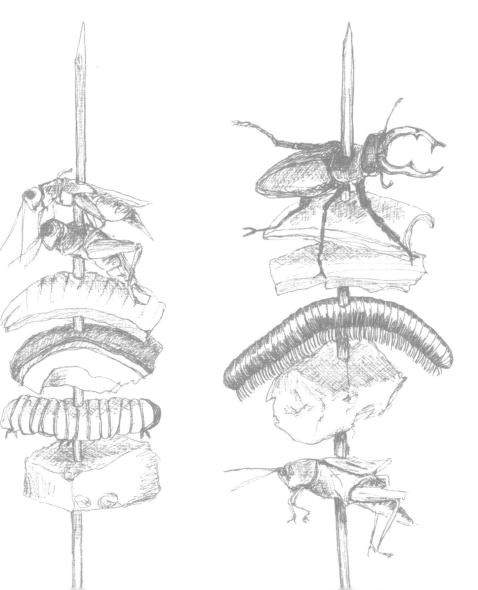

Index